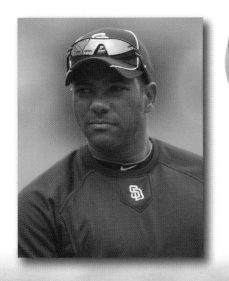

Baseball superstar!

2012

Plays for the Astros, the Orioles, the Padres, and the Giants.

2008-2011

Plays in the All-Star Game and is named MVP.

2004

Signs a contract with the Baltimore Orioles.

2003

Named Most Valuable Player.

2002

Plays his first game in the Major Leagues.

1997

Signs with the Oakland Athletics.

1993

Born in Baní in the Dominican Republic.

1976

Mason Crest
370 Reed Road
Broomall, Pennsylvania 19008
www.masoncrest.com

Printed and bound in the United States of America.

First printing
9 8 7 6 5 4 3 2 1

Library of Congress Cataloging-in-Publication Data

Rodriguez Gonzalez, Tania.
 Miguel Tejada / by Tania Rodriguez.
    p. cm.
Includes index.
ISBN 978-1-4222-2672-8 (hardcover) -- ISBN 978-1-4222-2670-4 (series hardcover) --
ISBN 978-1-4222-9161-0 (ebook)
 1. Tejada, Miguel, 1976---Juvenile literature. 2. Hispanic American baseball players--
Biography--Juvenile literature. 3. Baseball players--United States--Biography--
Juvenile literature. I. Title.
 GV865.T35R64 2012
 796.357092--dc23

 [B]

                                        2012021366

Produced by Harding House Publishing Services, Inc.
www.hardinghousepages.com

Picture Credits:
Keith Allison: p. 8
Luis Silvestre: p. 6
Mangin, Brad: p. 1, 2, 4, 7, 10, 12, 13, 14, 16, 18, 20, 21, 22, 24, 26, 28
All baseball card images courtesy of the Dennis Purdy collection.

MIGUEL TEJADA

Chapter 1

THE "GUAGUA"

I n the Dominican Republic, if you want to get to the other side of the island and back again, you would probably take a "guagua." Guaguas are privately owned minivans that go almost anywhere on the island. No matter how rusty and ramshackle they may look, you can count on them to bring you home.

Miguel Tejada knows all about guaguas. Today he's a *Major League Baseball* infielder who has played for the Oakland Athletics, the Baltimore Orioles, the Houston Astros, the San Diego Padres, and the San Francisco Giants—but he grew up in the Dominican Republic.

Tejada is a superstar in the baseball world, an amazing player with the ability to drive in runs. That's why his nickname is "La Guagua"—because his teammates know he can be counted on to drive them home!

Tejada has come a long way from his roots in the Dominican Repub-

lic—but it's those roots that helped him grow into the amazing player he is today. The island has a marvelous baseball *culture* that Tejada soaked up when he was still just a boy.

The History of Dominican Baseball

Historians aren't exactly sure how baseball first came to the island, but they know it's been there since at least 1880.

Americans brought the game of baseball to the Caribbean in the mid-1860s when U.S. business interests grew in Cuba, one of the Dominican Republic's neighbors. Then, between 1868 and 1878, many Cubans fled their country during their the Ten Years' War. Many of them ended up in the Dominican Republic. They brought the game of baseball with them—and it caught on fast!

The first Dominican baseball teams were formed either in the year 1894 or 1895. Eventually, strong teams took shape. These became the oldest baseball organizations in the country. They were the roots that grew into a thriving baseball culture.

The 1940s and the 1950s were good decades for Dominican baseball. The high point came in 1956, when the New York Giants *signed* Dominican infielder Ozzie Virgil. Virgil played for nine seasons in the

Dominican boys learn to love baseball when they're young. Miguel Tejada was once like these boys playing baseball wherever he could.

Tejada the baseball star found inspiration in other Dominican players like Ozzie Virgil, Manny Mota, and the Alou brothers.

American Major Leagues. He opened the door that Miguel Tejada and many others like him would eventually go through to find success in the American Major Leagues. Virgil showed the entire world that Dominicans were amazing baseball players.

Other Dominicans—Juan Marichal, the Alou brothers, Manny Mota, and others—helped open the door even wider to new baseball opportunities for young players like Tejada.

Everyone knew now that Dominican baseball players were some of the best in the world!

American leagues became very interested in the Dominican Republic. The leagues sent money, players, and **scouts** to the island. Dominican baseball players had the chance now to sharpen their skills against some of the world's best talent. Baseball schools opened across the island, offering boys the chance to learn to play ball. Some of these schools were

"La Guagua Dominicana."

good, some were bad. The best ones gave boys like Miguel Tejada the chance to make it big. Today, every team in Major League Baseball has a school or some other presence in the Dominican Republic. Baseball ties the United States and the Dominican Republic together.

Many baseball players from the Dominican Republic come to play in the United States. By 2011, a total of 420 players from the Dominican Republic had played in the Major Leagues. More Dominicans play in the Majors than players from any other country in Latin America. In fact, the Dominican Republic has more players in the Majors than all other countries in Latin America combined.

Today, the strength of Dominican baseball is found in each of the Major League's 30 teams. And at the same time, baseball is still just as popular on the island. Miguel Tejada and all the other Dominican players in the Majors inspire boys playing ball in the streets of the Dominican Republic. These boys dream about being the next A-Rod . . . or maybe Miguel Tejada. Players like Tejada make their country proud.

But Miguel Tejada, the Dominican "Guagua," was once like all the other boys growing up in the Dominican Republic, dreaming big dreams . . . never knowing his dreams would one day come true.

Dominican Coaches and Managers

Dominicans are leaving their mark on other aspects of the game as well. In 2003, Tony Peña, who once played for the Kansas City Royals, coached against Felipe Alou, of the San Francisco Giants, making it the first time that two Dominicans coached against each other in the Major Leagues. And then, in 2004, Omar Minaya became the first Dominican General Manager, working the front office for the New York Mets. Dominicans are first-class leaders in the world of baseball!

Chapter 2

THE BEGINNING

Miguel Tejada was born on May 25, 1976, in Baní in the Dominican Republic. Baní is a small city about 40 miles from Santo Domingo, the Dominican Republic's capital city.

Baní is a Native word meaning "abundant water." The area was named after an important leader of the first people who lived on the island, before the Spanish arrived.

After the Spanish came, they built settlements across the island, and in 1764, a group of neighbors who were worried about their safety came together to purchase a prop-

They Made It into a Book!

The story of Miguel Tejada's life, including his growing up years in the slums of Baní, is told in a book titled *Away Games: The Life and Times of a Latin Ballplayer* by Marcos Breton and José Luis Villegas. *Away Games* describes the struggles of Dominican players in general (as well as Tejada in particular) as they arrive in the United States speaking very little English. They often find themselves in small towns playing for minor league teams, far, far from the homes where they grew up, with only their dreams of making it big to give them hope.

erty large enough to build their own village in the valley of Baní. Banilejos (Baní citizens) are proud of their city's long history. They are well known for being industrious, successful businesspeople, and for having one of the best-kept towns in the Dominican Republic.

But Miguel Tejada did not grow up in the nicer areas of the city. Instead, for most of his life, his family lived in extreme poverty in the city's slums. Despite this, Miguel's childhood gave him riches of a different sort. One of the most important was the love of baseball that he learned from his family and from the neighborhood where he grew up. Like the rest of the Dominican Republic, Banijelos love baseball!

Miguel's mother's name was Mora, and his father's name was Daniel. He was the youngest of eleven children. His parents worked hard to support their large family, but in 1979, the family's small home and all their belongings were swept away by Hurricane David. The Tejadas had never been what you would call rich, but now they were forced to move to the slums at the edge of the city. There they lived in a rickety three-room shack with no running water or electricity.

Learning How to Work

As soon as he was old enough, Miguel went to work. He was begging at age three and shining shoes in the streets at age six. As he grew bigger, he helped his father on construction jobs. When his mother died in 1988, Miguel went to work in a clothing factory, earning only a few cents an hour.

Tejada's hero is former Baltimore Oriole Cal Ripken, Jr.

Who Is Cal Ripken, Jr.?

Cal Ripken, Jr. is one of the superstars of the baseball world. He won two MVP awards, set several fielding records, and helped the Baltimore Orioles win a World Series before retiring in 2001. He is famous for his powerful hits.

His family needed every penny they could get just to survive.

But Miguel's life wasn't all work. He spent his afternoons playing baseball. He learned the game from his brother, Juansito, a great player who might have made it big in the baseball world if he hadn't had a broken leg that healed badly. Miguel learned to be a strong hitter and a good fielder. He used a glove that had been made out of old milk cartons, but that didn't stop him from catching the ball!

Baseball was all Miguel thought about. Cal Ripken, Jr., the Baltimore Orioles' shortstop, was Miguel's idol, and Miguel dreamed of being just like Ripken when he grew up—a big-league shortstop.

Despite Miguel's big dreams, he didn't always look that good out on the field. He was clumsy sometimes, and some of the other boys teased him and told him he should give up. But Miguel had a good friend named Rafael Lugo—and sometimes a good friend can make all the difference in our lives. Whenever Miguel felt discouraged about his playing, Rafael persuaded him not to give up. Miguel made up his mind that he was going to make his dreams come true.

Miguel realized that the boys who drew the baseball scouts' attention were the ones who did something to make themselves stand out. A man named Enrique Soto, a former *minor leaguer* who had failed to reach the majors, told Miguel that most young Dominicans failed in the world of big-league baseball for the same reason Soto had—because they lacked the fundamentals. Soto and Miguel decided the best way for Miguel to succeed was to concentrate on the "little things" and show coaches he was eager to learn.

The Payoff

Miguel worked hard—and eventually his hard work paid off in an amazing way. When he was seventeen, he caught the eye of his country's great-

Since he was young, Tejada has worked hard to get better at baseball.

Miguel Tejada today.

est baseball hero, Juan Marichal. Now a scout for the Oakland A's, Marichal signed Miguel to the A's for $2,000. To Miguel, that seemed like a fortune!

Miguel entered Oakland's Dominican baseball school as just one of many boys hoping to become a shortstop in the Majors. The star of the school at the time was an outfielder named Mario Encarnación. Compared to Encarnación, Miguel barely even registered on the team's radar. But Miguel refused to be discouraged. He decided to take advantage of everything the school could offer him.

And baseball training wasn't the only thing the school offered Miguel. Throughout his entire life, Miguel had never had enough to eat—but now, for the first time, he did. He started to grow. He gained weight and strength in his upper body. His arms and legs became powerful.

Now when Miguel threw the ball, it zoomed across the infield. When he hit the ball, it seemed to jump off his bat. Slowly but surely, he rose up the charts. Finally, he was even better than the boys whom he had once looked up to.

And his big chance was about to come.

Chapter 3

PLAYING FOR THE OAKLAND ATHLETICS

Miguel began playing regularly in the Athletics' Dominican Summer League. He played second base and competed against players like José Jiménez, Timo Pérez and Carlos Febles—all of whom would one day be Major Leaguers. Miguel hit .294 with 18 homers and 62 *RBIs* in 74 games. This performance pushed him up to the top of the list in Oakland's Dominican complex. The team decided to send the 18-year-old to the United States for the 1995 season.

Playing in the Minor Leagues

Miguel's first year in the minors was with the Class-A Northwest League. While he played with the team, he stayed with a local family, Bobbi Naumes and her son, J.P., in southern Oregon.

This was a new experience for Miguel. He was amazed by how well Americans lived. He and J.P. got along like brothers, and Miguel had the chance to learn English. The only thing Miguel didn't like about living with the Naumes was their food! He missed the food he was used to eating in the Dominican Republic. Instead of sharing the Naumes' meals, he often fixed himself plates of beans and rice.

Although Miguel was sometimes homesick, he found that he didn't always have all that much in common with the other Latino players he met. They often did not share his drive to improve themselves. They seemed happy to go to the ballpark during the day and have fun at night. They didn't have the same sort of big dreams that Miguel did.

This was partly the fault of the teams for which they played. The teams often viewed the Latino players as simply a way to fill out their minor league rosters. The clubs didn't spend much time on the Latino players. The teams knew that one or two Latino players might prove to be good players—but they planned on eventually cutting the rest, replacing them from the fresh supply being trained back in the Caribbean. The players released from the team would be given a plane ticket home. Some players would cash in the ticket and simply melt into the general American population, living illegally in the States. They'd play ball on the weekends and try to get a job somewhere. Most of America would never learn their names.

Playing for the A's gave Tejada Major League experience.

Miguel made up his mind that he wouldn't be one of those players. He was determined to take advantage of the opportunity of being in the United States. He had his heart set on rising to the top.

His 1995 season was a good one. He was a dangerous hitter at bat and a solid fielder. And the Athletics were paying attention to his performance.

A Big-League Game

In 1996, Miguel had an amazing opportunity. While he was at the Athletics' training camp, he got a message telling him to get himself over to the big league complex. The team needed him to play shortstop for a Major League exhibition game.

Miguel was excited—but he didn't let his excitement hurt his performance. His hit a home run the first time he was up to bat!

The Number-One Prospect

His performance at the exhibition game got him assigned to the Athletics' California League, where many of the A's' best prospects played. Miguel proved he could handle it. At the plate, he hit everything the pitchers threw at him, and he had a powerful arm in the field.

The following season, 1997, Miguel ended up wearing the Huntsville uniform. The A's planned on giving him a full year in the Class-AA Southern League, where he could gain more experience. In 1998, they had decided to promote him to their top farm team.

But Miguel had such a good year with Huntsville that the A's changed their mind. They decided to skip the farm team—and send Miguel straight to the Majors!

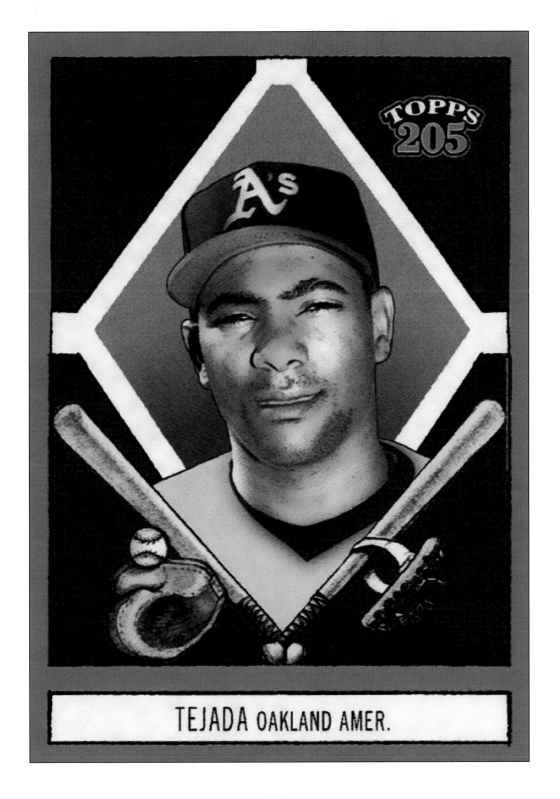

TEJADA OAKLAND AMER.

Chapter 4

THE MAJOR LEAGUES

Miguel Tejada played 26 games for the A's in September 1997, batting .202 in 99 at-bats and slugging a couple of home runs. His performance wasn't perfect, but his courage and enthusiasm impressed the club's managers.

The A's general manager, Billy Beane.

Managers Art Howe and Billy Beane didn't have a big budget—but they did have big plans for their team. They knew they didn't have the money to sign up multi-talented major leaguers. Instead, their strategy was to look for players who did one or two things really well—and then help them grow. Howe and Beane decided to take a chance with some *rookies* who looked like they could turn into major players—and Miguel Tejada was one of them.

The 1998 Season

Tejada didn't exactly fit the profile Howe and Beane were looking for, though. He still had a tendency to swing too often at bad pitches. He was still a young player with a lot to learn. Still, the A's experiment with Tejada was going well—until Miguel broke his middle finger of his right hand. The injury kept him out of the game until late in May. When he came back, he had a hard time keep his *batting average* higher than .200.

But Tejada was still working hard to improve his performance, just the way he always had ever since he was a boy. And he helped the A's improve their reputation as well during the 1998 season. They won 74 games, a respectable number.

1999

Howe and Beane were patient men— and in 1999 their patience paid off. The young players they'd taken a chance with—Jaha, Giambi, Stairs, Velarde, and Tejada—had some good years.

Miguel Tejada kept his batting average around .250. He finished the year with 21 home runs and 84 RBIs. And the A's finished 87-75, missing the *playoffs* by just three wins.

Tejada's performance on the field got better with every game.

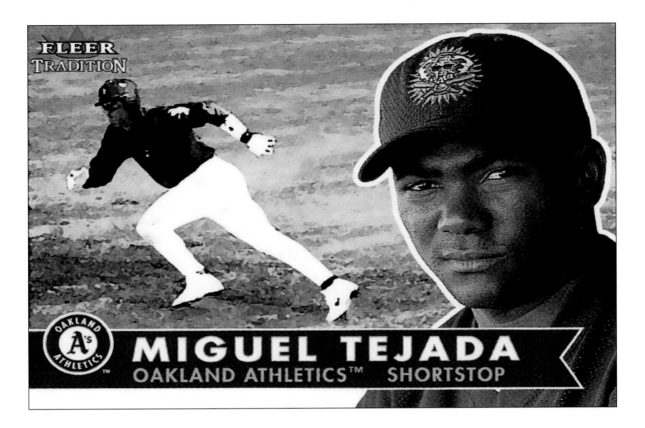

FLEER TRADITION

MIGUEL TEJADA
OAKLAND ATHLETICS™ SHORTSTOP

It Keeps Getting Better

Both the A's and Tejada were getting better and better. And 2000 was their break-through year. Tejada with Howe and Beane's core of young players lead the A's to their first American League Western *Division* win in eight years. Tejada's batting average was .275, and he hit 20 home runs. The A's won 91 games.

In 2001, Tejada hit .267 with 31 home runs. The A's captured the American League wild card with a 102–60 record. Howe and Beane's patience was finally paying off.

Break Through

The A's lost two of their key offensive players in 2002—Jason Giambi and Jermaine Dye—but Tejada was doing his best to make up for their loss. He hit .308 with 34 home runs—and he led the A's to their second Western Division title in three years. The team had a 20-game winning streak, and Tejada had done his part to make that happen. His great performance was rewarded with the 2002 American League *MVP* award.

2003

The next year, both the A's and Tejada got off to a slow start. Miguel hit under

Miguel played for the American League in one of his many All-Star Game appearances.

.200 during the first month of the season—but then things got better. Tejada hit .278 with 27 home runs, and the A's made their second straight Western Division title and their third in four years.

By the end of the 2003 season, Tejada had proved he was one of the best shortstops in the baseball world. Many of his dreams had come true.

But the following season would fulfill even more of his childhood dreams. At the end of the 2003 season, Tejada signed a six-year, $72 million **contract** with the Baltimore Orioles. Now Miguel would play for the same team as his childhood idol, Cal Ripken, Jr.

Who would have ever dreamed a boy from the slums of Baní could have risen so high?

Chapter 5

WHERE NEXT?

When Tejada arrived in Baltimore, he put on uniform number 10 for the first time. His old number with the A's—4—had been retired. But that didn't bother Miguel. He told reporters, "The good thing for me is I'm going to be walking in the same clubhouse that Cal Ripken walked in, and I'll have the same feeling. That's something that will make me do well for this team."

The Orioles were grateful to have him. They'd had some bad years, and they were looking to put some enthusiasm and excitement back into their team. "He gives you credibility right away," Orioles manager Lee Mazzilli said. "As a manager, you want to have a lineup that's out there every day. . . . That's the beauty of this kid—you've got to love him because he wants to play every day, every inning, all the time."

Tejada's willingness to give his best to the Orioles convinced other great players to join the team as well. Right-hander Sidney Ponson, for example, signed as a *free agent* in part because he knew the Orioles would be a better team with Tejada at shortstop. "He plays good *defense*, so he's going to help you a lot there," Ponson said. "He loves winning; a guy who plays with a lot of passion like that is great to have behind you."

The Orioles hoped Tejada would be their next Ripken—and Tejada was excited to have the chance. "For me," he said, "it's my dream come true to be on the same team as Cal Ripken, to be talking about him. It's making me real proud. . . . I know I'm going to mean a lot for this team. I hope everybody understands I'm not going to be the only one to go in the field. But I'll give 100 percent every day and play hard, and we're going to be a better team this year."

Dreams Can Come True

All of those hopes and dreams came true, at least for Tejada. He led the league with 150 RBIs in 2004. He also won the Century 21 Home Run Derby in July of that year. He hit a record 27 home runs in the contest.

The following year, he was an All-Star player. He won the All-Star MVP (and a Chevrolet Corvette).

But the Orioles were still struggling. They had losing season after losing season, and Tejada was losing faith in the team. He was unhappy with the team's direction, and he felt that the managers were not taking the action they needed to ensure the team's success. Tejada said, "I just want a good group that helps me win."

It didn't seem too much to ask—but Tejada didn't seem to be getting what he wanted. Meanwhile, he played in his one-thousandth consecutive game on July 1, 2006. Then he played another 152 games—and broke his wrist. On June 22, he was placed on the *disabled list*, ending the fifth longest streak in Major League history.

Superstars of Baseball: Miguel Tejada

Tejada had finished more than just his playing streak. He was also finished with the Orioles. He had given up on the team ever becoming what it had been when Cal Ripken, Jr. had played for it.

Tejada was ready to move to a new team. During 2008, he would play for the Houston Astros.

Tejada had a great year in Houston. He scored his thousandth career run that year. He played in the *All-Star Game*. He grounded 32 double plays, the most in the Major Leagues. Then in 2009, he again led the Majors in grounding double plays, this time with 29.

But the Orioles wanted him back. On January 23, 2010, Tejada signed a one-year, $6 million contract with the Baltimore Orioles. It looked like Tejada was going back to the team he had once loved so much.

The deal didn't work out, though, and in July, the Orioles *traded* him to the San Diego Padres. That year, while playing for the Padres, Tejada hit his 300th home run.

The following year, Tejada signed a one-year $6.5 million contract with the

Tejada played for the San Francisco Giants during the 2011 season.

Which Players Have the Longest Playing Streaks in Baseball History?

Cal Ripken, Jr.: 2,632 games
Lou Gehrig: 2,130 games
Everett Scott: 1,307 games
Steve Garvey: 1,217 games
Miguel Tejada: 1,152 games

San Francisco Giants. He batted .239 with only 26 RBIs in 91 games. The Giants weren't happy with his performance, and they released him at the end of the season.

Tejada Today

Miguel Tejada knew it was time to get back to what had always made him strong: his ability to work hard. He headed for Miami with a legendary workout trainer, Pete Bommarito. Tejada was determined to get his strength back. He made up his mind to become all he had once been. And by the end of the training season, rumors were getting around: Miguel Tejada had never looked better! Who knows what will come next for him?

Meanwhile, Tejada is staying true to his roots. He enjoys his family—his wife, Alejandra; his daughter, Alexa; and his son, Miguel, Jr. During the MLB offseason, he plays for the Dominican Winter League, the Águilas Cibaeñas. He's never forgotten the country where he grew up.

And baseball on the island is still going strong. The Dominican league now has six teams. The season begins in October and runs through February. Each teams plays 60 games, and the two finalists play for the championship. Both finalists also go on to represent the Dominican Republic in the Caribbean Baseball Series against Mexico, Venezuela, and Puerto Rico.

Miguel Tejada has done his part to show the world: Dominican baseball players are amazing!

Find Out More

Online

Baseball Almanac
www.baseball-almanac.com

Baseball Hall of Fame
baseballhall.org

Baseball Reference
www.baseball-reference.com

Dominican Baseball
mlb.mlb.com/mlb/features/dr/
index.jsp

History of Baseball
www.19cbaseball.com

Major League Baseball
www.mlb.com

Science of Baseball
www.exploratorium.edu/baseball

In Books

Augustin, Bryan. *The Dominican Republic From A to Z.* New York: Scholastic, 2005.

Jacobs, Greg. *The Everything Kids' Baseball Book.* Avon, Mass.: F+W Media, 2012.

Kurlansky, Mark. *The Eastern Stars: How Baseball Changed the Dominican Town of San Pedro de Macorís.* New York: Riverhead Books, 2010.

Glossary

All-Star Game: The game played in July between the best players from each of the two leagues within the MLB.

batting average: A statistic that measures how good a batter is, which is calculated by dividing the number of hits a player gets by how many times he is at bat.

contract: A written promise between a player and the team. It tells how much he will be paid for how long.

culture: The way of life of a group of people, which includes things like values and beliefs, language, food, and art.

defense: Playing to keep the other team from scoring; includes the outfield and infield positions, pitcher, and catcher.

disabled list: A list of players who are injured and can't play for a certain period of time.

division: A group of teams that plays one another to compete for the championship; in the MLB, divisions are based on geographic regions.

free agent: A player who does not currently have a contract with any team.

general manager: The person in charge of a baseball team, who is responsible for guiding the team to do well.

heritage: Something passed down by previous generations.

Major League Baseball (MLB): The highest level of professional baseball in the United States and Canada.

minor leagues: The level of professional baseball right below the Major Leagues.

Most Valuable Player (MVP): The athlete who is named the best player for a certain period of time.

offense: Playing to score runs at bat.

playoffs: A series of games played after the regular season ends, to determine who will win the championship.

professional: The level of baseball in which players get paid.

rookie: A player in his first-year in the MLB.

runs batted in (RBI): The number of points that a player gets for his team by hitting the ball.

scouts: People who find the best young baseball players to sign to teams.

sign: To agree to a contract between a baseball player and a team.

trade: An agreement with another team that gives a player in return for a player from the other team.

Index